STUDENT NAME:
YEAR/COLLEGE:
FORM TUTOR'S NAME:

HOW TO USE THIS LOG BOOK

STUDENTS

It is your responsibility to look after this logbook and take it with you to every lesson.
Write in your homework, tests, examinations, etc.
Keep your log book clean and tidy.
If you lose it, tell your Form Tutor immediately.

PARENTS

Please examine the log book carefully and check homework is being recorded.
We rely on parents to take an interest in their child's homework.
Please check that it has been completed on time and inform us of any problems.
Write any quick notes to Form Tutors on the day.

FORM TUTORS

Form Tutors will also regularly check this log book.

The School Day

SANDWICH
TECHNOLOGY
SCHOOL

Monday, Tuesday, Thursday, Friday

AM Registration/Assembly	**08.40 - 09.10**
Period 1	09.10 - 10.00
Period 2	10.00 - 10.50
MORNING BREAK	**10.50 - 11.10**
Period 3	11.10 - 12.00
Period 4a/Lunch 1	12.00 - 12.50
Period 4b/Lunch 2	12.50 - 13.40
PM Registration	**13.40 - 13.50**
Period 5	13.50 - 14.40
Period 6	14.40 - 15.30

Wednesday

AM Registration	**08.40 - 08.45**
Period 1	08.45 - 09.35
Period 2	09.35 - 10.25
Period 3	10.25 - 11.15
MORNING BREAK	**11.15 - 11.35**
Period 4	11.35 - 12.25
Period 5	12.25 - 13.15

(For students remaining in school)

LUNCH	13.15 - 14.00
Supported Study	14.00 - 15.30

SANDWICH TECHNOLOGY SCHOOL
TERMS AND HOLIDAYS – ACADEMIC YEAR 2021/2022

TERM 1 START:	**Thursday 2 September 2021**
FINISH:	**Friday 22 October 2021**
TERM 2 START:	**Monday 1 November 2021**
FINISH:	**Friday 17 December 2021**
TERM 3 START:	**Wednesday 5 January 2022**
FINISH:	**Friday 11 February 2022**
TERM 4 START:	**Monday 21 February 2022**
FINISH:	**Friday 1 April 2022**
TERM 5 START:	**Tuesday 19 April 2022**
BANK HOLIDAY:	**Monday 2 May 2022**
FINISH:	**Friday 27 May 2022**
TERM 6 START:	**Monday 6 June 2022**
FINISH:	**Tuesday 19 July 2022**

STAFF DEVELOPMENT DAYS:

Wednesday 1 September 2021;
Tuesday 4 January 2022;
Wednesday 20 July 2022 to Friday 22 July 2022 inclusive.

Week A

Monday A	Tuesday A	Wednesday A	Thursday A	Friday A
P1	P1	P1	P1	P1
P2	P2	P2	P2	P2
		BREAK		
P3	P3	P3	P3	P3
P4A	P4A	P4	P4A	P4A
P4B	P4B	P5	P4B	P4B
P5	P5		P5	P5
P6	P6		P6	P6

Week B

Monday B	Tuesday B	Wednesday B	Thursday B	Friday B
P1	P1	P1	P1	P1
P2	P2	P2	P2	P2
BREAK	BREAK	BREAK	BREAK	BREAK
P3	P3	P3	P3	P3
P4A	P4A	P4	P4A	P4A
P4B	P4B	P5	P4B	P4B
P5	P5		P5	P5
P6	P6		P6	P6

HOMEWORK TIMETABLE

	Week A		
	Subject	Subject	Subject
Mon			
Tues			
Wed			
Thurs			
Fri			

	Week B		
	Subject	Subject	Subject
Mon			
Tues			
Wed			
Thurs			
Fri			

Key School Staff Contacts

Headteacher: Mrs Tracey Savage

For all issues relating to students please contact the relevant Year team.

My Head of Year is:

My Year Manager is:

My Year Team Telephone Number is: (01304) 61_ _ _ _

My Tutor is:

Designated Safeguarding Lead is:
Mrs Wanstall (Deputy Headteacher) 01304 610103

Assistant Designated Safeguarding Lead is:
Mrs Kemp (Child Protection Officer) 01304 610044

Attendance Officer (attendance issues)
Mrs Mugford: 01304 610039
attendance@sandwich-tech.kent.sch.uk

SENCO
Mrs Judith Goodrich: 01304 610031
judith.goodrich@sandwich-tech.kent.sch.uk

Sandwich Sports and Leisure Centre
01304 614947

School website: www.sandwich-tech.kent.sch.uk

Conduct in School

We believe it is reasonable to expect that:
- nobody will be harassed, abused or harmed while at school
- teachers will be listened to and not interrupted when teaching
- students will be able to learn and not have their lessons ruined
- everyone will attempt the tasks that are set and ask for help politely if they are struggling
- everyone understands that rules are there to keep everyone safe and learning well so they do their best to follow them

Tips to stay safe online

There are lots of fun and interesting things you can do on the internet. And it can be a great way to stay in touch with friends. But it's important to understand how to stay safe online.

Sometimes people will try to trick you into clicking dangerous links or sharing things about yourself. Or something you've shared might be used to bully or frighten you.
- **Think before you post**
  Don't upload or share anything you wouldn't want your parents, carers, teachers or future employers seeing. Once you post something, you lose control of it, especially if someone else screenshots or shares it.
- **Don't share personal details**
  Keep things like your address, phone number, full name, school and date of birth private, and check what people can see in your privacy settings. Remember that people can use small clues like a school logo in a photo to find out a lot about you.
- **Watch out for phishing and scams**
  Phishing is when someone tries to trick you into giving them information, like your password. Never click links from emails or messages that ask you to log in or share your details, even if you think they might be genuine and never give out your password
- **Think about who you're talking to**
  There are lots of ways that people try to trick you into trusting them online. Even if you like and trust someone you've met online, never share personal information with them like your address, full name, or where you go to school.
- **Keep your device secure**
  Use strong passwords for accounts and cover your webcam as some viruses will let someone access your webcam without you knowing.
-

5 ways to get support if things go wrong
1. Talk to someone you trust like an adult, or you can always talk to a Childline counsellor
2. Report bullying and abuse directly to the website or app
3. Delete things you've shared that you're worried about, or find ways to hide them
4. Tell the police by making a report to CEOP if someone is threatening or blackmailing you
5. Plan for the future and change your privacy settings so it doesn't happen again

School Uniform

The school uniform enables students to feel part of our learning community. Students are expected to wear their uniform with pride at all times.

Basic dress:

Black long-sleeved jumper with school logo and college colour (red, green, yellow, blue)

Black unisex polo shirt with school logo and college colour
or
Black girls fit polo shirt with school logo and college colour

Black tailored straight legged school trousers, or black skirt, with logo.
No other skirts / trousers / leggings will be permitted.

Plain black school shoes **without** canvass or high heels (see school website for images of acceptable footwear)

Plain black coat of your choice (a 'hoodie' made from non-waterproof material is not acceptable). School coats with logos are available to purchase if preferred.

NO OTHER TOPS, TROUSERS OR SKIRTS WILL BE PERMITTED

Notes

- No fashion garments. Hats and scarfs should not be worn inside school buildings and coats should be removed in classrooms.
- Any make-up should be discreet.
- Jewellery is NOT allowed for Health & Safety reasons except a plain single stud for pierced ears. No other form of piercing is permitted.
- Hair should be in natural colours and in simple hair styles. Long hair should be tied back. Extraordinary hair styles including shaving patterns are unacceptable.
- Students are not permitted to wear acrylic nail extensions. Nails should be natural and a sensible length that will not affect participation in practical subjects. Only a clear polish can be worn if desired.

Students who fail to comply with these rules can expect to be sanctioned.

PE Kit:
- White polo top with school logo and college colour
- Optional long sleeve reversible black sports top with school logo
- Black/dark blue plain shorts or tracksuit trousers or sports leggings
- White sports socks (compulsory)
- Trainers (suitable for indoor and outdoor use)
  And
- Football boots (not compulsory but highly recommended for use on the field in winter)

Attendance

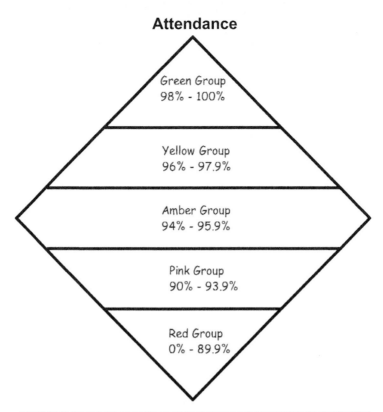

Attendance Groups	
Green	No risk
Yellow	Risk of underachievement
Amber	Serious risk of underachievement
Pink	Severe risk of underachievement
Red	Extreme risk – Court action

Attendance during one school year	Equals days absent	Which is approximately weeks absent	Which means the number of lessons missed	Absences over 5 years
95%	9 Days	2 Weeks	58 Lessons	0.25 Year
90%	19 Days	4 Weeks	116 Lessons	0.5 Year
80%	38 Days	8 Weeks	232 Lessons	1 Year
70%	57 Days	11.5 Weeks	333 Lessons	1.25 Years
60%	80 Days	16 Weeks	464 Lessons	2 Years
50%	100 Days	20 Weeks	580 Lessons	2.5 Years

Academic Progress

Subject	Target (Y11)	Progress 1			Progress 2			Progress 3		
		Prog.	ATL	HWK	Prog.	ATL	HWK	Prog.	ATL	HWK
English										
Maths										
Science										
History										
Geography										
Computer Science										
ICT										
Technology										
Art										
Drama										
Music										
PE										
SMSC										
Health										

Progress 1 Personal Targets

1) _____

2)_____

3)_____

Progress 2 Personal Targets

1) _____

2)_____

3)_____

Progress 3 Personal Targets

1) _____

2)_____

3)_____

Decide your future!

Finding it hard to decide what to do? We'll help you make decisions about your next steps at every stage. However, it's never too early to start looking yourself so have a look at these sources for help.

There is a careers page on the Sandwich Tech website. From the home page, select Careers from the 'Supporting Students' menu or go to: www.sandwich-tech.kent.sch.uk/192/careers

Select the useful links option to find out more about the following areas:

What are the options after year 11?
Find out about the 6th form, College options, Apprenticeships and Employment with training. Remember to aim high! The more grade 4s or higher you gain in your GCSEs, especially in Maths and English, the more options you have!

What jobs are out there?
There are several sites to explore to see descriptions and videos of jobs. It's fun to start researching and finding out what may interest you!

What type of career is right for you?
Have a go at a Careers quiz: Answer some simple questions and view job suggestions based on your interests, skills, qualities, and preferences. See the opportunities for work experience and volunteering: a great way to find out more about a career you are interested in.

What is University like?
Are you thinking about university as an option in the future? Have a look at what courses are available and what student life is like. The possibilities are endless!

What actually is an Apprenticeship?
Do you want to work and train at the same time? Perhaps an apprenticeship is for you. Find out about what an Apprenticeship actually is and the different opportunities available.

Do you want online careers guidance?
You have your own free Career portfolio (log in details available on the STS careers web page) which looks into career options for you. The great thing about it is that it stores your information and you can use and adjust it over your time at STS as your preferences and interests change and develop. It acts as an online personal careers document throughout your school career.

Don't forget there are lots of people you can talk to about your future steps and career: Subject teachers, form tutor, heads of year, family and friends. You can request a 1 to 1 meeting at any time with Mrs Rooke the School Careers Advisor who is based in the OLC.

Careers Activities

Many daily activities and events you participate in will help you gain skills for your career in the future, even if you don't know what you want to do yet. Keep a record of what you do and consider what skills you have gained from these activities and events (choose from the list below or add your own)

- Communication skills
- Team work
- Creativity
- Decision making
- Career awareness

- Organisational skills
- Time management
- Presentation skills
- Computer skills
- Public speaking

Activity	Detail	Skills gained
Member of a school team or club		
Participated in a school visit		
Participated in a careers activity		
Spoke to Mrs Rooke, the careers advisor, about my next steps and career ideas		
Joined a club outside of school		
Presented to my class		
Represented the school		
Work experience/part-time job		
Was part of a fundraising activity		
Participated in a visit/talk by an employer to STS		
Other:		

Well done! Remember you learn skills you will use for a career every day! Recall them for your CV or interviews!

Revision Techniques

Organisation

Before you can stat to revise, you need a suitable space and a plan. Your work space should be quiet, well-lit and free from distractions. That means not in front of the TV or computer! Turn your phone off or leave it in another room when you are revising to reduce the urge to check for new messages.

Draw up a revision timetable and stick to it. When planning this, be realistic with when you are revising and when you are doing it. Suggesting you will get up at 5am to revise for 2 hours before school is probably not realistic. You can find free timetable templates by searching the internet for "Revision Timetable Template".

Mind Maps

Mind maps help you to organise larger topics into smaller subtopics and their related ideas or key terms.

Teach a friend or family member

Einstein said "If you can't explain it simply – You don't know it well enough." By thinking about how to explain your work to someone else, you are engaging in active learning. This will deepen your understanding and help store those key facts in your long-term memory.

Recall and summarise your notes

After studying a topic, close your book and try to rewrite they key information from memory. Check it in your book and add in the missing points in a different colour pen. Repeat this over a longer period of time and see how your recall changes.

Flash Cards

Create your own flash cards with a question on one side and the answer on the other. You can then test your own knowledge or get someone else to test you. Great news is they don't need to know anything about the topic as the answer is right there!

Testing

Answering old exam questions is a great way to get used to exam style questions and how long you have to answer them. Using the mark schemes to check your answers allows you to see what the examiners were looking for. The more questions you do, the better you get an answering them.

Notes

Weekly Planner

September   *Septembre   Septiembre*   **Week: A**

Thursday 2nd   *Jeudi   Jueves*

Subject	Information	Due in	✓

Friday 3rd   *Vendredi   Viernes*

Subject	Information	Due in	✓

Notes

Weekly STARS		Tutor	

Never underestimate the power you have to take your life in a new direction. –
Germany Kent

September   *Septembre   Septiembre*   Week: B

Monday 6th   *Lundi   Lunes*

Subject	Information	Due in	✓

Tuesday 7th   *Mardi   Martes*

Subject	Information	Due in	✓

Wednesday 8th   *Mercredi   Miércoles*

Subject	Information	Due in	✓

Word of the week	**feign** v. to represent fictitiously; put on an appearance of Synonyms: fake, imitate, counterfeit

September   *Septembre   Septiembre*   Week: B

Thursday 9th   *Jeudi   Jueves*

Subject	Information	Due in	✓

Friday 10th   *Vendredi   Viernes*

Subject	Information	Due in	✓

Notes

Weekly STARS		Tutor	

This week in 1942, Enid Blyton published "Five on a Treasure Island" the first of the "Famous Five" series of novels. Have you read any of the series?

September   *Septembre   Septiembre*   Week: A

Monday 13th   *Lundi   Lunes*

Subject	Information	Due in	✓

Tuesday 14th   *Mardi   Martes*

Subject	Information	Due in	✓

Wednesday 15th   *Mercredi   Miércoles*

Subject	Information	Due in	✓

Word of the week

Abscond v. to depart in a sudden and secret manner, especially to avoid capture and legal prosecution

Synonyms: bolt, escape, flee   Antonym: remain

September   *Septembre   Septiembre*   **Week: A**

Thursday 16th   *Jeudi   Jueves*

Subject	Information	Due in	✓

Friday 17th   *Vendredi   Viernes*

Subject	Information	Due in	✓

Notes

Weekly STARS		Tutor	

Tip of the week: Think about where you are going to be able to study. Do you have a table away from distractions in your home? If not, think about where you can go to get your work done.

September *Septembre* *Septiembre*   **Week: B**

Monday 20th *Lundi* *Lunes*

Subject	Information	Due in	✓

Tuesday 21st *Mardi* *Martes*

Subject	Information	Due in	✓

Wednesday 22nd *Mercredi* *Miércoles*

Subject	Information	Due in	✓

Word of the week	**maverick** n. a person pursuing rebellious, even potentially disruptive, policies or ideas Synonyms: rebel, cowboy Antonym: conservative

September *Septembre   Septiembre*   **Week: B**

Thursday 23rd   *Jeudi   Jueves*

Subject	Information	Due in	✓

Friday 24th   *Vendredi   Viernes*

Subject	Information	Due in	✓

Notes

Weekly STARS		Tutor	

Hey diddle diddle! The median is the middle. You add, and then divide, for the mean. The mode is the most common one that you see, and the range is the difference between.

September   *Septembre*   *Septiembre*   Week: A

Monday 27th   *Lundi*   *Lunes*

Subject	Information	Due in	✓

Tuesday 28th   *Mardi*   *Martes*

Subject	Information	Due in	✓

Wednesday 29th   *Mercredi*   *Miércoles*

Subject	Information	Due in	✓

Word of the week	**umbrage** n. feeling of anger or annoyance caused by something offensive Synonyms: offence, annoyance Antonym: calmness

Thursday 30th *Jeudi   Jueves*

Subject	Information	Due in	✓

Friday 1st *Vendredi   Viernes*

Subject	Information	Due in	✓

Notes

Weekly STARS		Tutor	

Feeling sluggish, irritable and hungry in the afternoon lessons? Trade those sugary foods from break and lunch for healthy options like fruit.

October   *Octobre*   *Octubre*   Week: B

Monday 4th   *Lundi   Lunes*

Subject	Information	Due in	✓

Tuesday 5th   *Mardi   Martes*

Subject	Information	Due in	✓

Wednesday 6th   *Mercredi   Miércoles*

Subject	Information	Due in	✓

Word of the week	**controversial** adj. of, relating to, or characteristic of controversy, or prolonged public dispute or debate Synonyms: polemical, contentious Antonym: certain

October   *Octobre   Octubre*   **Week: B**

Thursday 7th   *Jeudi   Jueves*

Subject	Information	Due in	✓

Friday 8th   *Vendredi   Viernes*

Subject	Information	Due in	✓

Notes

Weekly STARS		Tutor	

This week in history – Thomas Edison showed his first motion picture in 1889
First transcontinental flight by a woman was completed by Laura Ingalls in 1930
We saw the far side of the Moon for the first time in 1959

October *Octobre Octubre*   Week: A

Monday 11th *Lundi Lunes*

Subject	Information	Due in	✓

Tuesday 12th *Mardi Martes*

Subject	Information	Due in	✓

Wednesday 13th *Mercredi Miércoles*

Subject	Information	Due in	✓

Word of the week	**repudiate** v. reject as having no authority or binding force Synonyms: abandon, dismiss, renounce Antonym: accept

October   *Octobre   Octubre*   **Week: A**

Thursday 14th   *Jeudi   Jueves*

Subject	Information	Due in	✓

Friday 15th   *Vendredi   Viernes*

Subject	Information	Due in	✓

Notes

Weekly STARS	**Tutor**

Tip for success: Turn off notifications on your phone and turn it off when you go to bed at night. This will help reduce the time you spend looking at the screen and help you to sleep better.

October   *Octobre   Octubre*   Week: B

Monday 18th   *Lundi   Lunes*

Subject	Information	Due in	✓

Tuesday 19th   *Mardi   Martes*

Subject	Information	Due in	✓

Wednesday 20th   *Mercredi   Miércoles*

Subject	Information	Due in	✓

Word of the week	**Succinct** adj. expressed with brevity and clarity, with no wasted words Synonyms: brief, concise Antonym: long-winded

October   *Octobre*   *Octubre*   **Week: B**

Thursday 21st   *Jeudi*   *Jueves*

Subject	Information	Due in	✓

Friday 22nd   *Vendredi*   *Viernes*

Subject	Information	Due in	✓

Notes

Weekly STARS		Tutor	

No matter how you feel, get up, dress up and show up. – Regina Brett

Monday 1st   *Lundi   Lunes*

Subject	Information	Due in	✓

Tuesday 2nd   *Mardi   Martes*

Subject	Information	Due in	✓

Wednesday 3rd   *Mercredi   Miércoles*

Subject	Information	Due in	✓

Word of the week	**dross** n. waste matter Synonyms: refuse, rubbish, dregs Antonym: assets

November   *Novembre   Noviembre*   **Week: A**

Thursday 4th   *Jeudi   Jueves*

Subject	Information	Due in	✓

Friday 5th   *Vendredi   Viernes*

Subject	Information	Due in	✓

Notes

Weekly STARS		Tutor	

Nothing is predestined. The obstacles of your past can become the gateways that lead to new beginnings. – Ralph Blum

November   *Novembre   Noviembre*   Week: B

Monday 8th   *Lundi   Lunes*

Subject	Information	Due in	✓

Tuesday 9th   *Mardi   Martes*

Subject	Information	Due in	✓

Wednesday 10th   *Mercredi   Miércoles*

Subject	Information	Due in	✓

Word of the week	**modicum** n. a moderate or small amount Synonyms: iota, ounce, shred Antonym: a lot

November   *Novembre   Noviembre*   **Week: B**

Thursday 11th   *Jeudi   Jueves*

Subject	Information	Due in	✓

Friday 12th   *Vendredi   Viernes*

Subject	Information	Due in	✓

Notes

Weekly STARS		Tutor	

This week in history - Gottfried Leibniz demonstrates integral calculus to find the area under the graph of y = f(x) in 1675
On the 11th hour of the 11th day of the 11th month, WWI ended in 1918.
Einstein and Szilard awarded a patent for the Einstein refrigerator in 1930.

November *Novembre   Noviembre*   Week: A

Monday 15th *Lundi   Lunes*

Subject	Information	Due in	✓

Tuesday 16th *Mardi   Martes*

Subject	Information	Due in	✓

Wednesday 17th *Mercredi   Miércoles*

Subject	Information	Due in	✓

Word of the week	**censorious** adj. severely critical Synonyms: fault finding, condemnatory, complaining Antonym: complimetary

November   *Novembre   Noviembre*   **Week: A**

Thursday 18th   *Jeudi   Jueves*

Subject	Information	Due in	✓

Friday 19th   *Vendredi   Viernes*

Subject	Information	Due in	✓

Notes

Weekly STARS		Tutor	

If you had to be trapped for a month in a children's book, which one would you chose?
Why not visit the library to discover new worlds to lose yourself in.

Monday 22nd   *Lundi   Lunes*

Subject	Information	Due in	✓

Tuesday 23rd   *Mardi   Martes*

Subject	Information	Due in	✓

Wednesday 24th   *Mercredi   Miércoles*

Subject	Information	Due in	✓

Word of the week	**pseudonym** n. a fictitious name used by an author to conceal their identity Synonyms: pen name, alias, nickname Antonym: name

November   *Novembre   Noviembre*   **Week: B**

Thursday 25th   *Jeudi   Jueves*

Subject	Information	Due in	✓

Friday 26th   *Vendredi   Viernes*

Subject	Information	Due in	✓

Notes

Weekly STARS		Tutor	

Times tables challenge week – Can you recite all your times tables up to 12x?
Do it each day and see how much you can improve over the week.

November-December   *Novembre   Noviembre*   Week: A

Monday 29th   *Lundi   Lunes*

Subject	Information	Due in	✓

Tuesday 30th   *Mardi   Martes*

Subject	Information	Due in	✓

Wednesday 1st   *Mercredi   Miércoles*

Subject	Information	Due in	✓

Word of the week	**oblivious** adj. unaware (usually followed by of or to) Synonyms: unmindful, unconscious of, inattentive Antonym: attentive

December   *Décembre   Diciembre*   **Week: A**

Thursday 2nd   *Jeudi   Jueves*

Subject	Information	Due in	✓

Friday 3rd   *Vendredi   Viernes*

Subject	Information	Due in	✓

Notes

Weekly STARS		Tutor	

Make sure you take regular exercise. It is proven to help raise self-esteem, help sleep problems, improve memory and concentration.

December   *Décembre   Diciembre*   Week: B

Monday 6th   *Lundi   Lunes*

Subject	Information	Due in	✓

Tuesday 7th   *Mardi   Martes*

Subject	Information	Due in	✓

Wednesday 8th   *Mercredi   Miércoles*

Subject	Information	Due in	✓

Word of the week	**languish** v. to be or become weak or feeble Synonyms: droop, fade, deteriorate Antonym: develop

December   *Décembre*   *Diciembre*   **Week: B**

Thursday 9th   *Jeudi*   *Jueves*

Subject	Information	Due in	✓

Friday 10th   *Vendredi*   *Viernes*

Subject	Information	Due in	✓

Notes

Weekly STARS		Tutor	

Tip for success:: Make to do lists. Prepare your to do list the night before. In doing so, you will know exactly what tasks you have to accomplish the next day.

December *Décembre* *Diciembre*   Week: A

Monday 13th *Lundi* *Lunes*

Subject	Information	Due in	✓

Tuesday 14th *Mardi* *Martes*

Subject	Information	Due in	✓

Wednesday 15th *Mercredi* *Miércoles*

Subject	Information	Due in	✓

Word of the week	**abject** adj. utterly hopeless Synonyms: miserable, humiliating, wretched Antonym: excellent

December   *Décembre   Diciembre*   **Week: A**

Thursday 16th   *Jeudi   Jueves*

Subject	Information	Due in	✓

Friday 17th   *Vendredi   Viernes*

Subject	Information	Due in	✓

Notes

Weekly STARS		Tutor	

Success is like wrestling a gorilla. You don't quit when you're tired. You quit when the gorilla is tired. – Robert Strauss

January   *Janvier   Enero*   **Week: B**

Wednesday 5th   *Mercredi   Miércoles*

Subject	Information	Due in	✓

Notes

Word of the week	**expendable** adj. considered to be not worth keeping or maintaining

Synonyms: disposable, unimportant, superfluous
Antonym: indispensable |

January   *Janvier*   *Enero*   **Week: B**

Thursday 6th   *Jeudi*   *Jueves*

Subject	Information	Due in	✓

Friday 7th   *Vendredi*   *Viernes*

Subject	Information	Due in	✓

Notes

Weekly STARS		Tutor	

Do not wait until the conditions are perfect to begin. Beginning makes the conditions perfect. – Alan Cohen

January   *Janvier   Enero*   **Week: A**

Monday 10th   *Lundi   Lunes*

Subject	Information	Due in	✓

Tuesday 11th   *Mardi   Martes*

Subject	Information	Due in	✓

Wednesday 12th   *Mercredi   Miércoles*

Subject	Information	Due in	✓

Word of the week	**semantic** adj. of, relating to, or arising from the different meanings of words or other symbols Synonyms: linguistic, syntactic

January   *Janvier   Enero*   **Week: A**

Thursday 13th   *Jeudi   Jueves*

Subject	Information	Due in	✓

Friday 14th   *Vendredi   Viernes*

Subject	Information	Due in	✓

Notes

Weekly STARS		Tutor	

Did you know that it was this week in 2007 that J.K.Rowling finished the final Harry Potter book?
Have you read them yet?
Visit the library to borrow a copy.

January   *Janvier   Enero*   **Week: B**

Monday 17th   *Lundi   Lunes*

Subject	Information	Due in	✓

Tuesday 18th   *Mardi   Martes*

Subject	Information	Due in	✓

Wednesday 19th   *Mercredi   Miércoles*

Subject	Information	Due in	✓

Word of the week	**jubilant** adj. showing great joy, satisfaction or triumph Synonyms: rejoicing, exultant Antonym: depressed

January *Janvier Enero*   **Week: B**

Thursday 20th *Jeudi* *Jueves*

Subject	Information	Due in	✓

Friday 21st *Vendredi* *Viernes*

Subject	Information	Due in	✓

Notes

Weekly STARS		Tutor	

This week in history – The first demonstration of an X-ray machine in 1896.
The first air raid on Britain in WWI occurred in 1915.
Edward the VIII became king in 1936.

January   *Janvier   Enero*   **Week: A**

Monday 24th   *Lundi   Lunes*

Subject	Information	Due in	✓

Tuesday 25th   *Mardi   Martes*

Subject	Information	Due in	✓

Wednesday 26th   *Mercredi   Miércoles*

Subject	Information	Due in	✓

Word of the week	**caustic** adj. capable of burning, corroding or destroying living tissue Synonyms: abrasive, acerbic, acidic Antonym: mild, soothing

January   *Janvier   Enero*   **Week: A**

Thursday 27th   *Jeudi   Jueves*

Subject	Information	Due in	✓

Friday 28th   *Vendredi   Viernes*

Subject	Information	Due in	✓

Notes

Weekly STARS		Tutor	

Tweedle-dee-deum and Tweedle-dee-dee,
Around the circle is pi times d,
But if the area is declared,
Think of the formula as π r squared.

Monday 31st   *Lundi   Lunes*

Subject	Information	Due in	✓

Tuesday 1st   *Mardi   Martes*

Subject	Information	Due in	✓

Wednesday 2nd   *Mercredi   Miércoles*

Subject	Information	Due in	✓

Word of the week	**lithe** adj. bending readily Synonyms: limber, supple, flexible Antonym: rigid

February   *Février*   *Febrero*   **Week: B**

Thursday 3rd   *Jeudi*   *Jueves*

Subject	Information	Due in	✓

Friday 4th   *Vendredi*   *Viernes*

Subject	Information	Due in	✓

Notes

Weekly STARS		Tutor	

Tip for success – Pack your bag the night before and ensure you have everything you need for the following day.

February *Février Febrero*　　　Week: A

Monday 7th　*Lundi　Lunes*

Subject	Information	Due in	✓

Tuesday 8th　*Mardi　Martes*

Subject	Information	Due in	✓

Wednesday 9th　*Mercredi　Miércoles*

Subject	Information	Due in	✓

Word of the week	**vex** v. irritate Synonyms: annoy, provoke, displease Antonym: appease

February   *Février   Febrero*   **Week: A**

Thursday 10th   *Jeudi   Jueves*

Subject	Information	Due in	✓

Friday 11th   *Vendredi   Viernes*

Subject	Information	Due in	✓

Notes

Weekly STARS		Tutor	

Forgiving others is not a weakness. It takes a strong person to forgive. –
Mufti Menk

February *Février   Febrero*   Week: B

Monday 21st *Lundi   Lunes*

Subject	Information	Due in	✓

Tuesday 22nd *Mardi   Martes*

Subject	Information	Due in	✓

Wednesday 23rd *Mercredi   Miércoles*

Subject	Information	Due in	✓

Word of the week	**garish** adj. crudely or tastelessly colourful, showy or elaborate, as clothes or decoration Synonyms: gaudy, ostentatious Antonym: drab

February   *Février*   *Febrero*   **Week: B**

Thursday 24th   *Jeudi*   *Jueves*

Subject	Information	Due in	✓

Friday 25th   *Vendredi*   *Viernes*

Subject	Information	Due in	✓

Notes

Weekly STARS		Tutor	

It's never too late to become who you want to be. I hope you live a life that you're proud of, and if you find that you're not, I hope you have the strength to start over. – The Curious Case of Benjamin Button

Monday 28th   *Lundi   Lunes*

Subject	Information	Due in	✓

Tuesday 1st   *Mardi   Martes*

Subject	Information	Due in	✓

Wednesday 2nd   *Mercredi   Miércoles*

Subject	Information	Due in	✓

Word of the week	**insinuate** v. to suggest, without being direct Synonyms: hint, indicate, intimate Antonym: declare

March   *Mars*   *Marzo*   **Week: A**

Thursday 3rd   *Jeudi*   *Jueves*

Subject	Information	Due in	✓

Friday 4th   *Vendredi*   *Viernes*

Subject	Information	Due in	✓

Notes

Weekly STARS		Tutor	

Tip for success: The key to learning something well is repetition; the more times you go over the material the better chance you have of storing it permanently.

Monday 7th *Lundi   Lunes*

Subject	Information	Due in	✓

Tuesday 8th *Mardi   Martes*

Subject	Information	Due in	✓

Wednesday 9th *Mercredi   Miércoles*

Subject	Information	Due in	✓

Word of the week	**affluent** adj. having an abundance of wealth, property or other material goods
	Synonyms: prosperous, rich Antonym: poor

March *Mars   Marzo*   Week: B

Thursday 10th   *Jeudi   Jueves*

Subject	Information	Due in	✓

Friday 11th   *Vendredi   Viernes*

Subject	Information	Due in	✓

Notes

Weekly STARS		Tutor	

This week in history – 1st GB census was carried out in 1801 recording 10m.
The first telephone call was made by Alexander Graham Bell in 1876.
First case of Spanish Flu, which killed 50-100 million, was documented in 1918.
Coronavirus declared a pandemic by WHO in 2020.

March   *Mars   Marzo*   **Week: A**

Monday 14th   *Lundi   Lunes*

Subject	Information	Due in	✓

Tuesday 15th   *Mardi   Martes*

Subject	Information	Due in	✓

Wednesday 16th   *Mercredi   Miércoles*

Subject	Information	Due in	✓

Word of the week	**nuance** n. a subtle difference or distinction in expression, meaning, response etc Synonyms: distinction, subtlety, refinement

March   *Mars*   *Marzo*   Week: A

Thursday 17th   *Jeudi*   *Jueves*

Subject	Information	Due in	✓

Friday 18th   *Vendredi*   *Viernes*

Subject	Information	Due in	✓

Notes

Weekly STARS		Tutor	

Cherry pies are delicious: Circumference = π diameter
Apple pies are too: Area = π r²

Monday 21st *Lundi Lunes*

Subject	Information	Due in	✓

Tuesday 22nd *Mardi Martes*

Subject	Information	Due in	✓

Wednesday 23rd *Mercredi Miércoles*

Subject	Information	Due in	✓

Word of the week	**caterwaul** v. to utter long wailing cries Synonyms: bawl, quarrel, screech Antonym: be quiet

March *Mars* *Marzo*   Week: B

Thursday 24th   *Jeudi*   *Jueves*

Subject	Information	Due in	✓

Friday 25th   *Vendredi*   *Viernes*

Subject	Information	Due in	✓

Notes

Weekly STARS		Tutor	

Literacy tip: Confused about the rule for adding s to words which end in a y?
If the word has a vowel before the final y (boy, day) just add s.
If the word has a consonant before the final y (baby, jelly) add ies.

Monday 28th   *Lundi   Lunes*

Subject	Information	Due in	✓

Tuesday 29th   *Mardi   Martes*

Subject	Information	Due in	✓

Wednesday 30th   *Mercredi   Miércoles*

Subject	Information	Due in	✓

Word of the week	**quintessential** adj. the purest or most perfect example of something
	Synonyms: typical, classic Antonym: abnormal

March-April *Avril Abril*   Week: A

Thursday 31st *Jeudi Jueves*

Subject	Information	Due in	✓

Friday 1st *Vendredi Viernes*

Subject	Information	Due in	✓

Notes

Weekly STARS		Tutor	

Success Is what comes after you stop making excuses. – Luis Galraza

April   *Avril   Abril*   Week: B

Monday 18th   *Lundi   Lunes*   Bank Holiday

Subject	Information	Due in	✓

Tuesday 19th   *Mardi   Martes*

Subject	Information	Due in	✓

Wednesday 20th   *Mercredi   Miércoles*

Subject	Information	Due in	✓

Word of the week	**mellifluous** adj. sweetly or smoothly flowing or sweet-sounding Synonyms: agreeable, harmonic, dulcet Antonym: discordant

April   *Avril   Abril*   **Week: B**

Thursday 21st   *Jeudi   Jueves*

Subject	Information	Due in	✓

Friday 22nd   *Vendredi   Viernes*

Subject	Information	Due in	✓

Notes

Weekly STARS		Tutor	

Challenges are gifts that force us to search for a new centre of gravity. Don't fight them. Just find a new way to stand. - Oprah Winfrey

Monday 25th   *Lundi   Lunes*

Subject	Information	Due in	✓

Tuesday 26th   *Mardi   Martes*

Subject	Information	Due in	✓

Wednesday 27th   *Mercredi   Miércoles*

Subject	Information	Due in	✓

Word of the week	**discordant** adj. being at variance Synonyms: disagreeing, clashing, jarring Antonym: similar

April *Avril   Abril*   **Week: A**

Thursday 28th   *Jeudi   Jueves*

Subject	Information	Due in	✓

Friday 29th   *Vendredi   Viernes*

Subject	Information	Due in	✓

Notes

Weekly STARS		Tutor	

Time magazine has published a list of 100 of the best young adult books of all time: https://time.com/100-best-young-adult-books/
How many have you read?
Why not increase that number by visiting the library and borrowing a book.

May *Mai* *Mayo*   # Week: B

Monday 2nd *Lundi* *Lunes*   Bank Holiday

Subject	Information	Due in	✓

Tuesday 3rd *Mardi* *Martes*

Subject	Information	Due in	✓

Wednesday 4th *Mercredi* *Miércoles*

Subject	Information	Due in	✓

Word of the week	**fraught** adj. filled or laden (with) Synonyms: replete, loaded Antonym: lacking

Thursday 5th   *Jeudi*   *Jueves*

Subject	Information	Due in	✓

Friday 6th   *Vendredi*   *Viernes*

Subject	Information	Due in	✓

Notes

Weekly STARS		Tutor	

This week in history – Christopher Columbus first sights Jamaica in 1494.
The Hindenburg disaster ends the age of Zeppelins in 1937.
The first postage stamp, the Penny Black, is used in Great Britain in 1840.
Margaret Thatcher becomes the first female prime minister of UK in 1979.

May *Mai* *Mayo*   Week: A

Monday 9th *Lundi* *Lunes*

Subject	Information	Due in	✓

Tuesday 10th *Mardi* *Martes*

Subject	Information	Due in	✓

Wednesday 11th *Mercredi* *Miércoles*

Subject	Information	Due in	✓

Word of the week	**baleful** adj. full of menacing influences Synonyms: pernicious, malevolent, evil Antonym: good

May   *Mai*   *Mayo*   **Week: A**

Thursday 12th   *Jeudi*   *Jueves*

Subject	Information	Due in	✓

Friday 13th   *Vendredi*   *Viernes*

Subject	Information	Due in	✓

Notes

Weekly STARS		Tutor	

Tip for success: Study more difficult subjects first and do the easier, more fun ones later.

Monday 16th   *Lundi   Lunes*

Subject	Information	Due in	✓

Tuesday 17th   *Mardi   Martes*

Subject	Information	Due in	✓

Wednesday 18th   *Mercredi   Miércoles*

Subject	Information	Due in	✓

Word of the week	**incoherent** adj. without logical or meaningful connection Synonyms: disjointed, rambling Antonym: intelligible

May   *Mai*   *Mayo*   **Week: B**

Thursday 19th   *Jeudi*   *Jueves*

Subject	Information	Due in	✓

Friday 20th   *Vendredi*   *Viernes*

Subject	Information	Due in	✓

Notes

Weekly STARS		Tutor	

Speed = distance ÷ time
Can you rearrange this equation to make distance or time the subject?
Did you know this is a formula you need to know for both maths and science?

Monday 23rd   *Lundi   Lunes*

Subject	Information	Due in	✓

Tuesday 24th   *Mardi   Martes*

Subject	Information	Due in	✓

Wednesday 25th   *Mercredi   Miércoles*

Subject	Information	Due in	✓

Word of the week	**opulent** adj. wealthy, rich or affluent Synonyms: deluxe, extravagant, lavish Antonym: economical

May   *Mai*   *Mayo*   **Week: A**

Thursday 26th   *Jeudi*   *Jueves*

Subject	Information	Due in	✓

Friday 27th   *Vendredi*   *Viernes*

Subject	Information	Due in	✓

Notes

Weekly STARS		Tutor	

Treat others as you would like to be treated yourself. – Matthew 7:12

June *Juin* *Junio*   Week: B

Monday 6th *Lundi* *Lunes*

Subject	Information	Due in	✓

Tuesday 7th *Mardi* *Martes*

Subject	Information	Due in	✓

Wednesday 8th *Mercredi* *Miércoles*

Subject	Information	Due in	✓

Word of the week	**attribute** n. a quality, property or characteristic of somebody or something Synonyms: facet, trait

June   *Juin*   *Junio*

Week: B

Thursday 9th   *Jeudi*   *Jueves*

Subject	Information	Due in	✓

Friday 10th   *Vendredi*   *Viernes*

Subject	Information	Due in	✓

Notes

Weekly STARS		**Tutor**	

You may have a fresh start any moment you choose, for this thing that we call 'failure' is not the falling down, but the staying down. – Mary Pickford

June   *Juin   Junio*   Week: A

Monday 13th   *Lundi   Lunes*

Subject	Information	Due in	✓

Tuesday 14th   *Mardi   Martes*

Subject	Information	Due in	✓

Wednesday 15th   *Mercredi   Miércoles*

Subject	Information	Due in	✓

Word of the week	**sedate** adj. undisturbed by passion or excitement Synonyms: calm, serene, composed Antonym: agitated

June   *Juin   Junio*   **Week: A**

Thursday 16th   *Jeudi   Jueves*

Subject	Information	Due in	✓

Friday 17th   *Vendredi   Viernes*

Subject	Information	Due in	✓

Notes

Weekly STARS		**Tutor**	

This week in history – The Magna Carter was signed by King John in 1215.
The British defeat Napoleon and France at the Battle of Waterloo in 1812.
Robert Bunsen invents the Bunsen burner in 1847.
Anne Frank begins her diary in 1942.

June *Juin Junio*   Week: B

Monday 20th *Lundi Lunes*

Subject	Information	Due in	✓

Tuesday 21st *Mardi Martes*

Subject	Information	Due in	✓

Wednesday 22nd *Mercredi Miércoles*

Subject	Information	Due in	✓

Word of the week	**reverberate** v. to echo or resound Synonyms: rebound, re-echo, ring Antonym: quieten

Thursday 23rd   *Jeudi   Jueves*

Subject	Information	Due in	✓

Friday 24th   *Vendredi   Viernes*

Subject	Information	Due in	✓

Notes

Weekly STARS		Tutor	

Tip for success: Find a study method that suits you. Make notes, use diagrams, flow charts and mind maps. Experiment and find what works for you.

Monday 27th *Lundi Lunes*

Subject	Information	Due in	✓

Tuesday 28th *Mardi Martes*

Subject	Information	Due in	✓

Wednesday 29th *Mercredi Miércoles*

Subject	Information	Due in	✓

Word of the week	**elicit** v. to draw or bring out or forth Synonyms: educe, evoke, extract Antonym: give

June-July   *Juillet   Julio*   **Week: A**

Thursday 30th   *Jeudi   Jueves*

Subject	Information	Due in	✓

Friday 1st   *Vendredi   Viernes*

Subject	Information	Due in	✓

Notes

Weekly STARS		Tutor	

Fancy finding a new book for the summer holidays?
Check out the award winners for the year:
https://www.waterstones.com/category/cultural-highlights/book-awards
Try something that is different from your usual books.

July *Juillet Julio*   Week: B

Monday 4th *Lundi   Lunes*

Subject	Information	Due in	✓

Tuesday 5th *Mardi   Martes*

Subject	Information	Due in	✓

Wednesday 6th *Mercredi   Miércoles*

Subject	Information	Due in	✓

Word of the week	**incisive** adj. remarkably clear and direct Synonyms: sharp, keen, acute Antonym: weak

July   *Juillet   Julio*   **Week: B**

Thursday 7th   *Jeudi   Jueves*

Subject	Information	Due in	✓

Friday 8th   *Vendredi   Viernes*

Subject	Information	Due in	✓

Notes

Weekly STARS		Tutor	

"Learning is a treasure that will follow its owner everywhere"
Chinese proverb

July   *Juillet   Julio*   **Week: A**

Monday 11th   *Lundi   Lunes*

Subject	Information	Due in	✓

Tuesday 12th   *Mardi   Martes*

Subject	Information	Due in	✓

Wednesday 13th   *Mercredi   Miércoles*

Subject	Information	Due in	✓

Word of the week	**plethora** n. a large or excessive amount of something Synonyms: excess, abundance, surfeit Antonym: lack

July *Juillet Julio*   # Week: A

Thursday 14th *Jeudi   Jueves*

Subject	Information	Due in	✓

Friday 15th *Vendredi   Viernes*

Subject	Information	Due in	✓

Notes

Weekly STARS		Tutor	

Tip for success: If you get distracted when studying, write your thoughts on a pad and return to them later.

July   *Juillet   Julio*   **Week: B**

Monday 18th   *Lundi   Lunes*

Subject	Information	Due in	✓

Tuesday 19th   *Mardi   Martes*

Subject	Information	Due in	✓

Notes

Weekly STARS		Tutor	

"There will come a time when you believe everything is finished; that will be the beginning." – Louis L'Amour

The Periodic Table of the Elements

Key

atomic number
Symbol
name
relative atomic mass

(1)	(2)											(3)	(4)	(5)	(6)	(7)	(0)
1 **H** hydrogen 1.0																	2 **He** helium 4.0
3 **Li** lithium 6.9	4 **Be** beryllium 9.0											5 **B** boron 10.8	6 **C** carbon 12.0	7 **N** nitrogen 14.0	8 **O** oxygen 16.0	9 **F** fluorine 19.0	10 **Ne** neon 20.2
11 **Na** sodium 23.0	12 **Mg** magnesium 24.3											13 **Al** aluminium 27.0	14 **Si** silicon 28.1	15 **P** phosphorus 31.0	16 **S** sulfur 32.1	17 **Cl** chlorine 35.5	18 **Ar** argon 39.9

		(3)	(4)	(5)	(6)	(7)	(8)	(9)	(10)	(11)	(12)						
19 **K** potassium 39.1	20 **Ca** calcium 40.1	21 **Sc** scandium 45.0	22 **Ti** titanium 47.9	23 **V** vanadium 50.9	24 **Cr** chromium 52.0	25 **Mn** manganese 54.9	26 **Fe** iron 55.8	27 **Co** cobalt 58.9	28 **Ni** nickel 58.7	29 **Cu** copper 63.5	30 **Zn** zinc 65.4	31 **Ga** gallium 69.7	32 **Ge** germanium 72.6	33 **As** arsenic 74.9	34 **Se** selenium 79.0	35 **Br** bromine 79.9	36 **Kr** krypton 83.8
37 **Rb** rubidium 85.5	38 **Sr** strontium 87.6	39 **Y** yttrium 88.9	40 **Zr** zirconium 91.2	41 **Nb** niobium 92.9	42 **Mo** molybdenum 95.9	43 **Tc** technetium	44 **Ru** ruthenium 101.1	45 **Rh** rhodium 102.9	46 **Pd** palladium 106.4	47 **Ag** silver 107.9	48 **Cd** cadmium 112.4	49 **In** indium 114.8	50 **Sn** tin 118.7	51 **Sb** antimony 121.8	52 **Te** tellurium 127.6	53 **I** iodine 126.9	54 **Xe** xenon 131.3
55 **Cs** caesium 132.9	56 **Ba** barium 137.3	57–71 lanthanoids	72 **Hf** hafnium 178.5	73 **Ta** tantalum 180.9	74 **W** tungsten 183.8	75 **Re** rhenium 186.2	76 **Os** osmium 190.2	77 **Ir** iridium 192.2	78 **Pt** platinum 195.1	79 **Au** gold 197.0	80 **Hg** mercury 200.6	81 **Tl** thallium 204.4	82 **Pb** lead 207.2	83 **Bi** bismuth 209.0	84 **Po** polonium	85 **At** astatine	86 **Rn** radon
87 **Fr** francium	88 **Ra** radium	89–103 actinoids	104 **Rf** rutherfordium	105 **Db** dubnium	106 **Sg** seaborgium	107 **Bh** bohrium	108 **Hs** hassium	109 **Mt** meitnerium	110 **Ds** darmstadtium	111 **Rg** roentgenium	112 **Cn** copernicium		114 **Fl** flerovium		116 **Lv** livermorium		

UK & Ireland

Europe

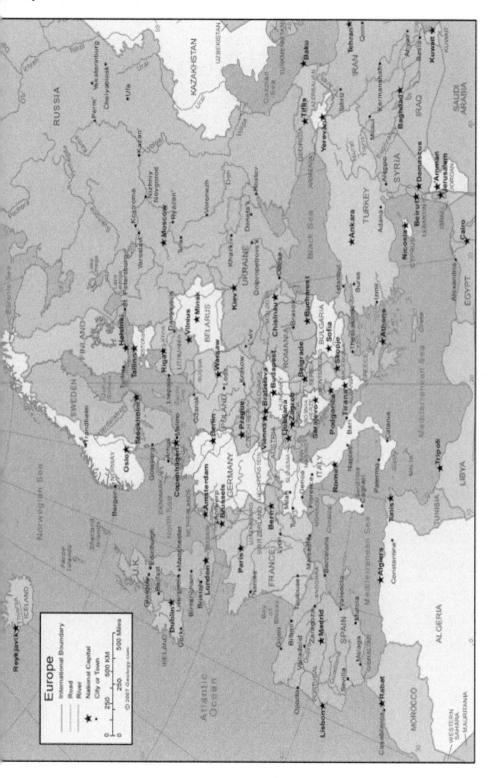

World

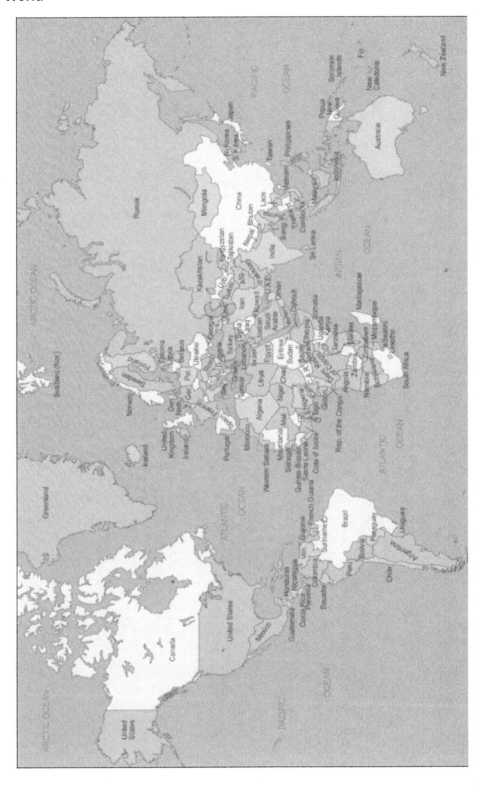

Science Formulae

Density (kg/m^3) = Mass (kg) ÷ Volume (m^3)

Distance (m) = Speed (m/s) x Time (s)

Acceleration (m/s^2) = Change in Velocity (m/s) ÷ Time (s)

Kinetic Energy (J) = 0.5 x Mass (kg) x Speed^2 (m/s)

Force (N) = Mass (kg) x Acceleration (m/s^2)

Momentum (kgm/s) = Mass (kg) x Velocity (m/s)

Work Done (J) = Force (N) x Distance (m)

Power (W) = Work Done (J) ÷ Time (s)

Force exerted by a spring (N) = Extension (m) x Spring Constant (N/m)

Gravity Force (N) = Mass (kg) x Gravitational Field Strength, g (N/kg)

Potential Energy (J) = Mass (kg) x Height (m) x Gravitational Field Strength, g (N/kg)

Pressure (Pa) = Force normal to a surface (N) ÷ Area of surface (m^2)

Moment of a force (Nm) = Force (N) x Distance (m)

Charge Flow (C) = Current (A) x Time (s)

Potential Difference (V) = Current (A) x Resistance (Ω)

Energy Transferred (J) = Charge (C) x Potential Difference (V)

Power (W) = Potential Difference (V) x Current (A) = Current^2 (A) x Resistance (Ω)

Energy Transferred (J, kWh) = Power (W, kW) x Time (s, h)

Wave Speed (m/s) = Frequency (Hz) x Wavelength (m)

Efficiency = Useful output energy transfer (J) ÷ Input energy transfer (J)

Maths Formulae

Areas

Rectangle = l x w	
Parallelogram = b x h	
Triangle = ½b x h	
Trapezium = ½ (a + b) h	
Curved Surface Area of a Cylinder = 2 x π x radius x height	
Curved Surface Area of a Cone = π r l	

Volumes

Cuboid = l x w x h	
Prism = area of cross section x length	
Cylinder = $\pi r^2 h$	
Pyramid = $\frac{1}{3}$ x area of base x h	
Sphere = $\frac{4}{3}$ x π x radius^3	

Circles

Circumference = π x diameter C = πd	
Circumference = 2 x π x radius C = 2πr	
Area of a circle = π x radius squared $A = \pi r^2$	
Area of a Sector = $\dfrac{\text{Angle} \times \pi \times \text{radius}^2}{360}$	
Arc length = $\dfrac{\text{Angle} \times \pi \times \text{diameter}}{360}$	

Pythagoras

Pythagoras' Theorem For a right-angled triangle, $a^2 + b^2 = c^2$	
Trigonometric ratios Sin $x^\circ = \dfrac{\text{opp}}{\text{hyp}}$, cos $x^\circ = \dfrac{\text{adj}}{\text{hyp}}$, tan $x^\circ = \dfrac{\text{opp}}{\text{adj}}$	

Compound Measures

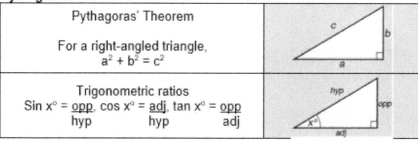

Speed = Distance ÷ Time	
Density = Mass ÷ Volume	
Pressure = Force ÷ Area	

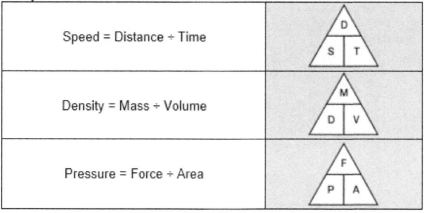

Midpoint of two points

Between (x_1, y_1) and (x_2, y_2) the midpoint is:

$$\left(\frac{x_1 + x_2}{2}, \frac{y_1 + y_2}{2}\right)$$

Gradient of a Line

$$m = \frac{y_2 - y_1}{x_2 - x_1}$$

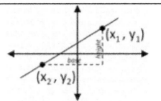

(x_1, y_1)

(x_2, y_2)

Compound Interest

$$\text{starting amount} \times \left(1 \pm \frac{rate\ of\ change}{100}\right)^{time}$$

The ± means:
+ for growth
- for decay

Perpendicular Gradients

Flip & Swap

To find the perpendicular gradient, find the reciprocal, and switch signs.

$$m = -\frac{1}{m}$$

The Quadratic Equation

The solutions of $ax^2 + bx + c = 0$,
Where $a \neq 0$, are given by:

$$x = \frac{-b \pm \sqrt{(b^2 - 4ac)}}{2a}$$

Median from a histogram

$$L + \frac{m - p}{f} \times w$$

L is the lower limit of the median class
m is the median point
p is the total frequency of the previous bars
f is the frequency of the median class
w is the class width of the median class

Probability

Where *P(A)* is the probability of outcome *A* and *P(B)* is the probability of outcome *B*:

$$P(A\ or\ B) = P(A) + P(B) - P(A\ and\ B)$$

Constructing Pie Charts

The angle to draw for each sector is:

$$\text{Angle} = \frac{frequency}{total} \times 360°$$

Stratified Sampling

$$\frac{\text{frequency of group}}{\text{total}} \times \text{sample size}$$

Interior/Exterior Angles

Exterior: $\dfrac{360}{n}$ Interior: $180 - \text{exterior}$

Sum of interior: $(n - 2) \times 180$

Trigonometric Exact Values

	Sin θ	Cos θ	Tan θ
0°	0	1	0
30°	$\dfrac{1}{2}$	$\dfrac{\sqrt{3}}{2}$	$\dfrac{\sqrt{3}}{3}$
45°	$\dfrac{\sqrt{2}}{2}$	$\dfrac{\sqrt{2}}{2}$	1
60°	$\dfrac{\sqrt{3}}{2}$	$\dfrac{1}{2}$	$\sqrt{3}$
90°	1	0	$\pm\infty$

Trigonometric Formulae

Sine Rule $\dfrac{a}{\sin A} = \dfrac{b}{\sin B} = \dfrac{c}{\sin C}$

Cosine Rule $a^2 = b^2 + c^2 - 2bc \cos A$

Area of triangle $= \dfrac{1}{2} ab \sin C$

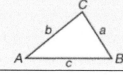

Out of Lesson Log

Date	Time	Teacher

Date	Time	Teacher

Date	Time	Teacher

Printed in Great Britain
by Amazon